FIFTH EDITION

Green Building Guidelines

Meeting the Demand for Low-Energy, Resource-Efficient Homes

Library of Congress ISBN Number: 0976207354
Library of Congress Control Number: 2007920431